MOVING CONTINENTS
Our Changing Earth

Thomas G. Aylesworth

—an Earth Processes book—

ENSLOW PUBLISHERS, INC.

Bloy St. & Ramsey Ave.	P.O. Box 38
Box 777	Aldershot
Hillside, N.J. 07205	Hants GU12 6BP
U.S.A.	U.K.

Library of Congress Cataloging-in-Publication Data

Aylesworth, Thomas G.
  Moving continents: our changing earth / by Thomas G. Aylesworth
        p. cm. —(An Earth processes book)
  Includes index.
  Summary: Describes the theory of plate tectonics and the various forces that
continue to change the surface of the earth. Discusses the history of the theory as well
as evidence that seems to dispute it.
  ISBN 0-89490-273-3
  1. Plate tectonics—Juvenile literature. 2. Continental drift—Juvenile literature.
3. Geology, Structural—Juvenile literature.
  [1. Plate tectonics. 2. Continental drift. 3. Geology.]
  I. Title. II. Series.
QE511.4.A95 1990
551.1'36—dc20

                                                                              89—33549

Printed in the United States of America

10 9 8 7 6 5 4 3 2 1

Illustration Credits:
Virginia Aylesworth, pp. 6, 32, 36, 38 (top), 40, 44, 46, 47, 48, 50; Virginia
Aylesworth (after Wegener), pp. 13, 14, 15; California Historical Society, p. 33;
NASA, p. 52; U. S. Geological Survey, pp. 28, 38 (bottom).

Cover Photo:
Lyn Topinka, U.S.G.S./CVO

Contents

Acknowledgments

The author would like to thank the following people who helped so much on the preparation of this book: Christopher Carr, who edited it; Jeffrey C. Callister, Newburgh Free Academy, Newburgh, N.Y., and Sharon Stroud, Widefield High School, Colorado Springs, Colo., who critiqued the manuscript; and Isabel S. Grossner, who copyedited it.

1

Iceland—A Country in Motion

It was a normal August day. The temperature was about 10° C (50° F). The beautiful day was cloudless. The landscape gave us the impression that we were on the moon. We were in Iceland—a land of stark beauty and amazing contrasts. It is a land where the red lava of brooding black volcanoes contrasts with the freezing white glare of the glacial ice.

We had left Reykjavíc, the capital city, and had driven for miles, past huge greenhouses filled with vegetables growing indoors with the aid of heat taken from hot rocks below the surface, past vast bleak lava beds without a speck of green for miles. We had seen the Great Geyser, with its column of boiling water spouting to more than 150 feet (45.7 meters). We had seen Gullfoss, the beautiful "golden waterfall," and its ever-present sparkling rainbow, where thousands of tons of icy water thunder majestically down double falls into a deep gorge.

And then we arrived at Thingvellir, or the Parliament Plains— one of the most historic and sacred places in Iceland. There, in a great amphitheater of lava, the Icelandic nation was founded in A.D. 930. In the olden days, the Icelanders would meet there in summer to pass laws, make legal decisions, and celebrate the end of winter. And there is where we had one of the most eerie and breathtaking experiences of our lives—each placing one foot on one plate and the other on another plate.

According to the theory of plate tectonics, the earth's surface is made up of a series of pieces, or sections, called plates, that are continually moving. Most of North America is located on what is called the North American plate, and most of Europe and Asia is located on the Eurasian plate. Separating these two plates is the Mid-Atlantic Ridge which, for the most part, runs along the bottom of the Atlantic Ocean. Since it is the boundary between the two moving plates, this ridge is constantly under stress.

But the ridge is not completely underground. Because of its rapid growth, it has risen to the surface in Iceland, where it has formed a rift zone (a rift is a gap in the surface of the earth). These

The great Gullfoss waterfall in Iceland.

great open tensional cracks are best observed at Thingvellir, and to stand straddling one of them is mind-boggling. The thought that between one's feet is a line that is formed at the point at which two mighty conflicting plates meet is overwhelming, and even frightening. We couldn't get over the thought that any moment the plates might split and that would be the end of us.

Iceland—that ever-changing island—is referred to in tourist leaflets as a country of "plate tectonics in action." A forked volcanic zone divides the island where the two plates part company. New fissures (narrow openings in a rock caused by tension or pressure that pulls the rock apart) open every few months. Before an eruption, the pressure can lift the ground level near the volcano as much as 3.3 feet (1 meter). Since the Mid-Atlantic Ridge is spreading the surrounding area, the area of Iceland is also increasing. Brand-new islands have been rising from the sea as a result of volcanic activity off Iceland. One of these was Surtsey, which rose from the sea south of Heimaey in 1963. So great is the volcanic activity of Iceland that in many places the Icelanders have run water pipes through the new lava from volcanoes to supply their central heating.

The idea that the crust of the earth has not always been the same and that perhaps some of the continents were once attached to each other dates back a long time. Perhaps the first important thinker to notice that the coastlines of western Africa and eastern South America looked as though they matched was the English philosopher, Francis Bacon. This was in 1620. Bacon felt it was hardly accidental that they were so similar, but he offered no explanation.

In the 1650s a Frenchman named François Placet suggested that the Old World and the New World had first been split apart by the great flood described in the Bible. More than a hundred years later, Benjamin Franklin, that great American scientific investigator, had an idea that contained the seed of a theory that the surface of the earth is floating. He wrote that the earth has a spherical core that is surrounded by fluids that support a rocky outer layer.

Still, it was a long time before anyone advanced a real theory about our drifting continents. And to understand this, we need to look at what our earth seems really to be like.

2

Our Earth—Its Structure and History

Scientists now have a pretty good idea of the structure of the earth. We can't, of course, look directly inside our planet, since light doesn't travel through rock. But scientists who have studied earthquake waves have given us a hint about what might be found beneath the surface.

As these waves pass through rock, their speed and direction change as the rocks change. So geologists (scientists who study the earth—its composition, origin, history, and the processes that alter it, such as streams and glaciers) can probe the rocks deep in the earth's interior by measuring how long it takes earthquake waves to travel from an earthquake to various points around the globe.

What this has revealed is that the earth is made up of layers, something like an egg. On the outside is a thin crust. This crust, as compared to the thickness of the whole planet, is about the same as the thickness of postage stamps stuck all over a basketball. Under the crust is a mantle, which makes up more than 82 percent of the volume of the earth. Below that is a very dense and hot core.

The cool, rigid skin of the earth, consisting of the crust and the uppermost part of the mantle, is called the lithosphere (from the Greek *lithos*, or stone). This layer is about 60 miles (100 kilometers) deep. Scientists and engineers have never been able to remove rock samples by drilling any deeper than 7.5 miles (12 kilometers), and that was from the world's deepest hole, in the Kola peninsula in the Soviet Union.

Just below the lithosphere in the mantle is the asthenosphere (from the Greek *asthenos*, or lack of strength, or plastic). In this area the rocks are partly melted by radioactive heat produced by the radioactive decay of such elements as uranium and radium, and may even flow. The depth of the asthenosphere is about 124 miles (200 kilometers). Below the asthenosphere, also in the mantle, is the mesosphere (from the Greek *mesos*, or middle). Its depth is about 1,550 miles (2,500 kilometers). Because of the greater pressure, the rocks here are more rigid.

Below the mesosphere, extending to the center of the earth, is the core. The outer part of the core, about 1,370 miles (2,200 kilometers) deep, is liquid. The center of the core is solid, and is about 790 miles (1,270 kilometers) wide.

But back to the crust, where the drifting continents are found. In the continental areas, we find that the elements silicon, aluminum, calcium, magnesium, and iron are most common. These elements, combined with oxygen, make up the most common rock—granite. Below the oceans the crust consists mostly of basaltic rock containing these same elements. Because it contains more iron and magnesium than the granite, however, the basalt is denser.

While the best present guess about the mantle is that it consists largely of oxygen, silicon, aluminum, calcium, magnesium, and iron, as we have just said, the core is probably made up of iron, nickel, and several other metallic elements. It is the metals of the core that create the earth's magnetic makeup.

Geologists often liken the earth's outer shell to a cracked hard-boiled egg. It is broken into a number of rocky plates which slide on top of the much softer lower layer of the asthenosphere. Because the plates move as rigid bodies, their boundaries change constantly as they grind against each other. These motions and collisions have made vast changes on the face of the earth in the passage of a great deal of time. Scientists have ideas about what has happened to the earth in some billions of years.

The age of the oldest rocks that we know of can be estimated to go back to the Precambrian era, perhaps 3.8 billion years ago. At that time our planet was more molten that it is today. A large number of volcanoes were present on the surface, and they emitted gases and lava.

During the Precambrian era, the continents were perhaps only one-eighth of their present size. There was no life on the land and only microscopic life in the seas. The atmosphere was unbearable for most forms of life, having no free oxygen and too much carbon dioxide. The sun blasted ultraviolet light unfiltered by an ozone layer onto the earth's surface. The days were much shorter than twenty-four hours because the planet was rotating much faster then. The moon would have looked much larger, since its orbit was much closer to the earth than it is today.

In the latter part of the Precambrian period, the continents had become almost as large as they are today. In the meantime, microscopic plants were creating oxygen in the seas through the process we know as photosynthesis. The continents were drifting together and became a supercontinent (about 1 billion years ago) that did not break up until about 700 million years ago.

About 570 million years ago the earth entered our own era—the Paleozoic (the time of abundant forms of life). In the first period of this era, the Cambrian, most of the landmasses lay around the equator. There had been an explosion of life in the sea.

One reason for the birth of so many new life forms was that

there was more free oxygen in the ocean. Another was that the greatly spreading seafloor caused midocean ridges under the sea to grow. As they got bigger, the ridges occupied more space under the water and caused the water to rise and cover lowlands on the surface. That created vast warm shallow seas which could support more and more species of living things.

About 500 million years ago, the earth entered the next period of the Paleozoic era—the Ordovician. Europe and North America were beginning to close the Iapetus Ocean—the proto-Atlantic Ocean. Offshore island chains collided first and crumpled the continental shelf into peaks. Some of the eroded remains of these islands became the Green Mountains of Vermont.

Then came the Silurian period of the Paleozoic era, about 435 million years ago. The ozone layer in the upper atmosphere had grown dense enough to block most of the ultraviolet light from the sun. Many kinds of plants had already moved onto the land. By the next period, the Devonian, about 400 million years ago, the animals had followed the plants onto the land. The first trees appeared and became abundant in the lowlands. Primitive insects, scorpions, and spiders were in these forests, being eaten by the earth's first amphibians.

About 325 million years ago, the earth was in the middle of the Carboniferous period. North America and Europe were lying across the equator. Part of Africa was colliding with part of North America, creating the southern and central Appalachian Mountains. Meanwhile, some of the fresh-water ice lying over the South Pole was melting. This caused constant flooding of the continents, and forests flourished.

The warm moist conditions created a perfect climate for the amphibians as well as for the formation of coal. Coal is formed when vegetation grows so fast that it buries dead layers before they can decay. The dead vegetation is then sealed in by the sediment from rivers and acted upon by deep interior heat and pressure.

Then came the Permian period, about 290 million years ago. With the exception of what is now China, all the continents had come together in a single landmass called Pangaea. Collision had made the Appalachian Mountains extremely high. This prevented the rainfall from passing over the mountains and turned what was to become the northwest part of the United States into deserts and grasslands. Similar species that once inhabited separate continents were forced to share one landmass and compete for survival.

Thousands of land and sea animals became extinct during the Permian period, but those animals who could cope with the new situation were able to endure. For example, reptiles, who lay hard-shelled eggs, could live farther away from bodies of water than their amphibian ancestors, who lay soft-shelled eggs.

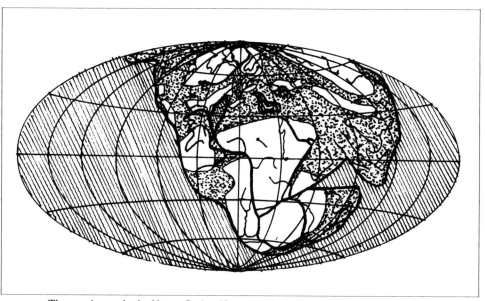

The continents in the Upper Carboniferous period (about 300 million years ago). Dotted areas represent regions underwater.

By the Triassic period, about 240 million years ago, most of the landmass was drifting north. The land was warming up and the glaciers were melting. Early dinosaurs, marine reptiles, and small mammals began to appear.

The Jurassic period began about 205 million years ago, and the large landmass had already begun splitting apart. As what was to become New England pulled away from what was to become Morocco, the Atlantic Ocean began forming.

Then came the Cretaceous period, about 138 million years ago. The separation of the continents continued. By the late Cretaceous period, the seas had risen almost 1,600 feet (500 meters) above their present level. Only about 15 percent of the surface of the earth was above sea level. During this time, trillions of tiny plants, called plankton, died and sank to the seafloor to turn into petroleum in somewhat the same way that coal was formed.

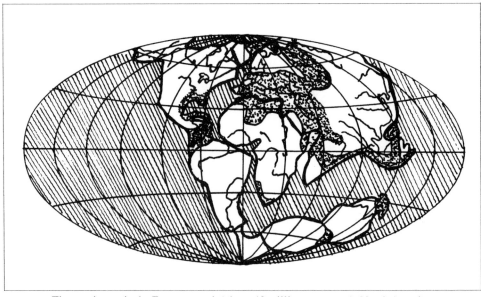

The continents in the Eocene epoch (about 40 million years ago). North America, part of South America, Antarctica, and Australia have begun to split.

At the end of the Cretaceous period, the dinosaurs—the lords of the earth since the late Triassic period—were dead. Many theories have been advanced to explain their disappearance, and the argument is still going on. It could have been due to a worldwide change in climate, the impact of a monstrous meteor, or a combination of several factors. But it seems to have happened about 65 million years ago.

With the dinosaurs gone, the earth entered the Cenozoic period—the age of mammals. The continents were still drifting apart and the animal populations were being isolated on separate continents where they developed in separate ways. Each continent soon became home to different families of life. North America had mastodons, tapirs, early camels, and early meat-eaters. South America harbored armadillos, giant sloths, and many marsupials (pouched animals related to kangaroos and koalas).

About 3 million years ago, colliding ocean floors raised the

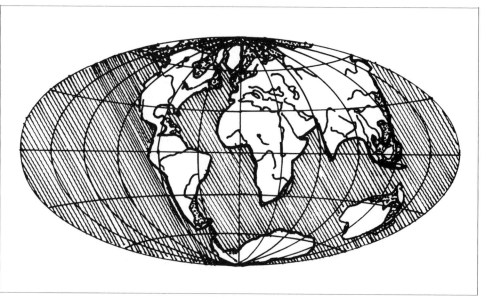

The continents in the Older Quaternary period (about 2 million years ago). They have now almost reached their present positions on the globe.

Isthmus of Panama between the Americas, and animals became able to migrate across this land bridge in both directions. Some of them, such as the armadillo, were successful in their new homes, but others could not survive the competition. About 2 million years ago, a new creature appeared in Africa—*Homo habilis*—the first human.

3

Continental Drift—
An Idea Is Born

The suggestion by Francis Bacon about the curious "jigsaw puzzle" of the continents began to interest investigators in the late 1700s. It was then that a new breed of scientists called geologists began to turn old notions about the earth upside down. Reading the records left in rocks, they realized that oceans had once covered what is now dry land and that glaciers had advanced and retreated across northern Eurasia and the Americas. This was to lead to the theory that the geographical features of our planet's surface are constantly changing—one of the great insights of the human mind.

In the early 1800s, the German natural philosopher (that is what scientists were called in those days) Karl Wilhelm von Humboldt suggested that the Old World and the New World might once have been joined. The Atlantic Ocean, he suggested, had the structure of a valley created by the separation of South America and Africa.

Later in the nineteenth century, scientists found fossils of a reptile from the Permian period, Mesosaurus, on both sides of the South Atlantic Ocean. Since this animal couldn't have swum

17

across the ocean, how did it exist on both sides? These scientists came up with the idea of a prehistoric land bridge.

Throughout that century, many discoveries of identical rock layers and fossils in widely distant countries puzzled geologists. Some of them had found traces of unusual sand and gravel and scratched rocks in the tropics. These were certainly laid down by glaciers, but what were glaciers doing in the tropics? They found prehistoric desert sands in rainy areas. What was desert sand doing there? There were ancient coal forests in the Arctic region. If coal is formed from ancient trees, how was it made in the treeless Arctic? In the early 1900s a British expedition found plant fossils a mere 400 miles (644 kilometers) from the South Pole. All these discoveries, and many more, led to the theory that there had been great shifts in climate all over the surface of the earth.

Scientists were intrigued anew by the idea that continents seemed to have mirror-image boundaries. They noticed how similar the eastern edge of North America is to the western edge of Europe and the northwestern edge of Africa. These two

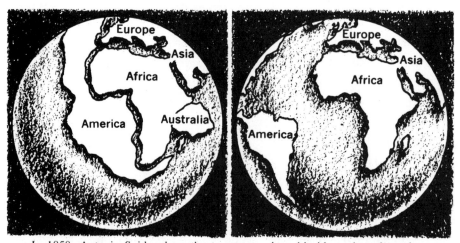

In 1858, Antonio Snider drew these maps to show his ideas about how the continents have drifted. His explanation was that at the time of the flood described in the Bible, there was a great outpouring of material from within the earth that rifted and pushed the continents apart, forming the Atlantic Ocean.

landmasses looked as if they would nestle together like the parts of a giant jigsaw puzzle. They also saw that the eastern border of South America could fit in with the southern three-quarters of the coast of Africa. If India were attached to the southwestern edge

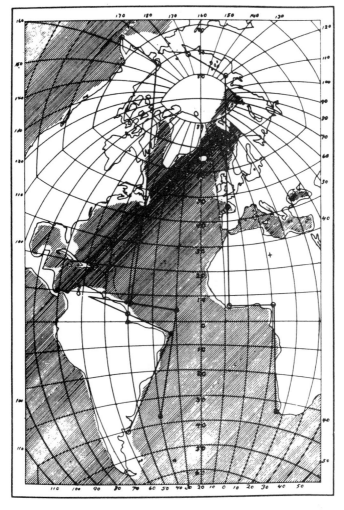

A diagram made in 1907 by W.H. Pickering. It shows how the Atlantic coastlines are parallel. The straight lines near South America suggest that the continent has rotated clockwise a few degrees while drifting away from Africa.

of Africa, with Australia to its south, and if Antarctica bordered the tip of Africa, the western coast of India, and the western border of Australia, the jigsaw puzzle would be complete. The whole map would look like a huge supercontinent.

The first step toward a modern viewpoint was made by a German meteorologist and geophysicist named Alfred Wegener. He first outlined his theory in 1912 in a paper called "The Origin of Continents." He refined the theory in 1915 in his book, *The Origin of Continents and Oceans*.

Wegener realized that the east coast of South America would fit neatly into the west coast of Africa only if the Atlantic Ocean were closed. He also knew of the mysterious fossils and climates that other scientists had described. And he knew about the newly discovered geological information, the similarity of rocks of

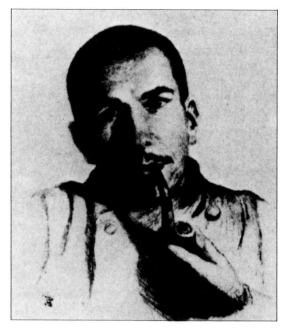

Alfred Wegener at the age of twenty-seven.

various ages and compositions on each side of the Atlantic. When the coastlines were fitted together, the geology matched.

He came up with the idea of a supercontinent he called Pangaea, which he thought might have existed some 300 million years ago. About 200 million years ago, he argued, some unknown force split this mass into separate continents. He suggested that fragments drifted slowly through the earth's mantle more or less the way ice floes drift through water. He said that North America was moving westward relative to Europe at about 10.5 inches (32 centimeters) per year.

Wegener's theory was first called continental displacement, but that name was later changed to continental drift. Like many other revolutionary ideas, Wegener's created a tempest among the learned people of his day. Those who agreed with him came up with the theory that Pangaea broke up into two gigantic landmasses. One (they named it Gondwanaland) was made up of what is today South America, Africa, India, Australia, and Antarctica. The other (they called it Laurasia) was made up of what was to become North America and Europe.

Most scientists, however, disbelieved Wegener and ridiculed him openly. There was no way of explaining how these masses had broken up to form the continents as they were known then and as we know them today. It is difficult to explain a force so strong that it can move continents. After all, the smallest continent, Australia, weighs 1,200 million million million pounds (500 million million million kilograms).

Harold Jeffrys was one of the prominent geophysicists who challenged the theory of continental drift. He pointed out that the idea of a solid stone continent plowing its way through the solid stone ocean floor defied the laws of physics. Wegener had first thought that North and South America were being forced westward by tidal forces in the crust of the earth. Jeffrys pointed out that if these tidal forces were strong enough to move continents, they would also be strong enough to stop the eastward rotation of the earth.

Wegener countered by suggesting the theory of "flight from the poles" (which he called *polflucht*). He suggested that this force was created by the earth's rotation and had caused India to migrate from the Antarctic into Southeast Asia, thereby heaving up the Himalayan Mountains. But then Jeffrys used mathematics to show that such a force could not move continents because the earth's crust was too strong.

Still, a portion of the geological community was taking continental drift seriously by the 1920s. Nevertheless, no one could identify a mechanism that could move continents, and most scientists were skeptical. In 1930 Wegener went to Greenland, where he had done meteorological field work twice before. He died there in a blizzard—his theory still largely unaccepted. The scientific world was split into "mobilists" and "fixists," but the fixists were in the majority. It was another twenty years before the theory was considered seriously again.

4

Plate Tectonics—A New Idea

In the 1950s, scientists once more became interested in the idea of continental drift. In the 1940s, early echo-sounding devices, the ancestors of modern sonar (an ocean depth-finding instrument), had located many flat-topped seamounts (undersea mountains taller than 3,300 feet, or 1,000 meters) on the floor of the ocean. These seamounts were called guyots, and were found to be the remains of volcanic islands that may have been flattened by the action of the surf. The problem was that no one could figure out how they got so far below sea level.

In the 1950s, rocks and fossils found in ocean basins, once considered to be very ancient (perhaps even part of the earth's original crust), were found to be surprisingly young. At least, they were young compared to the 4.6 billion-year-old earth itself. Besides, the layers of deep-sea sediment were much thinner than they would have been had they accumulated over billions of years. So part of the earth's crust was not all that ancient.

The essentials of what was to become plate tectonics were first outlined in 1960 in a paper titled "An Essay in Geopoetry." It was written by Harry Hess, a professor of geology at Princeton University and a rear admiral in the United States Naval Reserve.

He suggested that the earth's mantle is a plastic solid (something like Silly Putty). The hot rocks of the mantle rise in huge convection currents at the rate of about 0.4 inch (1 centimeter) per year under the mid-ocean ridges, which are globe-circling mountain chains that snake some 40,000 miles (64,360 kilometers) along the floors of the seven seas—propelled by a convection current. A convection current is a circular current caused by the movement of heated material through a liquid or a gas. Colder, denser material sinks, causing warmer, less dense material to rise. This effect can be seen in a home heating system. When warm air enters a room, it rises. As it rises, it cools and returns to the floor.

When these currents reach the lithosphere, they spread outward in both directions from the midocean ridges, and they push along, not only the plates, but also the continents riding as passengers on the plates. This process, called seafloor spreading by the marine geologist Robert Dietz, was the missing mechanism that drift theorists had been looking for. But it still required some discoveries about the magnetic property of the earth to clear matters up.

The earth has a strong magnetic field, but its origin has puzzled scientists throughout the ages. Although the ancient Chinese and Greeks knew something about our planet's magnetic field, it was not until the 1960s that scientists began to understand the nature of that field.

An English physicist and physician, William Gilbert (1540–1603), suggested that the earth behaves like an enormous bar magnet. His theory was believed until this century. Then scientists discovered that at roughly every 200,000 to 300,000 years, the earth's magnetic poles reverse: north becomes south and south becomes north. Such reversals contradict the idea of a permanent bar magnet and its fields.

Over the last thirty years or so an explanation has been developed. As the earth spins on its axis, the fluid layer of the outer core lets the mantle and solid lithosphere rotate somewhat faster than the solid inner core. According to some geologists, this allows the electrons in the outer core, mantle, and crust to move faster than those in the inner core. This sets up a natural "electric" dynamo that forms an associated magnetic field similar in shape to the field of a bar magnet.

Once geologists could measure very low-strength magnetic fields, they had a valuable research tool. Many rocks contain small quantities of iron. When these rocks were formed, the particles of iron acted as tiny compasses and settled in the direction of the earth's magnetic field at that time. The magnetic orientations of these minerals provided clues to the reversals of the magnetic field.

The study of ancient magnetism held another clue for geologists. The magnetic field of the earth is stronger at the magnetic poles than at the magnetic equator, and this affects the exact angle at which particles of iron are magnetized. By measuring the direction and dip angle of the magnetic field in a rock, geologists could determine the latitude on the face of the earth at which the rock originally was formed. Comparing this with the present latitude of the rock, they could build up a record of how landmasses have rotated and moved relative to each other.

Harry Hess's theory of a spreading seafloor was that convection forced molten rock, known as magma, to well up within the earth's mantle and to crack the lithosphere above. As the magma cooled, it formed a strip of rock which gradually spread out as more magma flowed from the crack. The great midocean ridges were the site of this activity.

Many scientists would not accept the theory that the seafloor is spreading until they were faced with the data from magnetic surveys in the 1960s. Scientists on research ships had measured the magnetism of rocks across ocean ridges such as the Mid-Atlantic Ridge. They found that the rocks on the ocean floor were magnetized in alternate directions in a series of bands parallel to the ridges. Moreover, the pattern of bands was identical on both sides of a ridge.

They explained this by saying that when lava from the mantle cools into rock on the ocean floor, it is magnetized in the direction of the magnetic field at that time. As the lava continues to erupt, it cracks the previous strip of newly solidified rock, splitting it in two. If the magnetic field reverses, then this next strip of rock will be magnetized in the opposite direction to the previous strip and will form a band in between.

This evidence, together with the increasing age of the rocks as the researchers moved away from the ridges, supported the idea of seafloor spreading. It showed how, as the midocean ridges continually added material to the ocean floors, continents once joined could become separated by huge oceans.

In 1965, a Canadian geophysicist, J. Tuzo Wilson of the University of Toronto, brought together the ideas of continental drift and seafloor spreading into a single global concept of moving areas and rigid plates. He had studied ancient rocks, and in his research he found that these rocks did not have the same magnetic "fix" toward the north and south magnetic poles as younger rocks.

The older the rock, he found, the more its magnetism deviated from true north. And the deviation could be as great as 30. Wilson guessed that this meant that the landmasses were once in different places on the globe. He also pointed out that running down the middle of the undersea mountain range called the Mid-Atlantic Ridge, there is a rift valley. The Mid-Atlantic Ridge runs along the bottom of the Atlantic Ocean, and the rift is the point where convection currents emerge from the earth's mantle. Could these heat currents have forced the continents apart? Rock specimens from this rift are often thirty times younger than the average age of most rocks on the continents.

Wilson believed that the Indian Ocean was formed by the separation of Africa, India, Australia, and Antarctica. Some Australian scientists have estimated that their continent is 3,400 miles (5,471 kilometers) farther from North America than it was 100 million years ago. The whole continent seems to be drifting at a rate of 2 inches (5 centimeters) per year. And scientists in Iceland have discovered that the farther away from a fault (a crack in rocks in which the sides move against each other) in the rift valley of the Mid-Atlantic Ridge, the older the rocks are likely to be.

At the same time, some scientists disagreed with the theory. For example, Dr. H. W. Menard of Scripps Institute of Oceanography in La Jolla, California, discovered that the geography of the bottom of the Pacific Ocean is a great deal different from that of the Atlantic. He asked whether, if convection currents have forced the Old World and the New World apart, wouldn't there be some similar mountains and midocean ridges in the Pacific?

Early in 1967, geophysicists in the United States added another idea—that of underthrusting, that one block of crustal material dips beneath another at deep-sea trenches. From such ideas, British, French, and U.S. scientists conceived a grand theory of the earth's lithosphere. The theory soon took on the name of plate tectonics (the word "tectonics" comes from the Greek word meaning builder). The idea was that the outer layer of the earth, the lithosphere, consists of six or more major plates which move over the hot, partially molten asthenosphere. As plates move, they bump into each other, move apart, and slide past each other, carrying the oceans and continents with them.

The key idea in plate tectonics is that the surface of the earth exists in a state of equilibrium of size or volume. Thus the earth is not growing larger or shrinking. Plates can grow at midocean ridges where heat and magma rise from the asthenosphere to form new oceanic lithosphere. This is balanced by a type of underthrusting, or subduction, as it is now called, melting plates elsewhere returning older lithosphere to the asthenosphere. That is, new plate is formed as magma rises and cools to rock by upward convection, and old plate is returned to the "melting pot" by downward convection.

Plate tectonics not only supported Wegener's theory, it revolutionized geology. In addition to revising textbooks on earth science, the new theory cast light on seemingly unrelated questions. Why do climates shift? Where did metals come from? Why did some species die off and others change?

Data gathered by scientists using laser and satellite techniques now show that the various plates are moving between 0.6 and 2.8 inches (1.5 and 7 centimeters) per year. This is about the same speed at which your fingernails grow. The plates that meet at the Mid-Atlantic Ridge, for example, are moving apart by about 0.78 inches (2 centimeters) a year on average.

Plate tectonics provides a global framework that successfully explains many of the structural and geophysical phenomena on the earth's surface—from mountain building and earthquakes to continental drift.

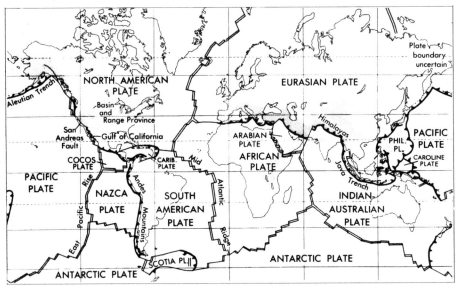

Lithosphere plates of the earth.

Although our knowledge of the earth's outer layer is incomplete, the following explanation is what we think is happening.

We think of the earth's surface as a thin skin stretched over a hot interior. The outer surface of rocks rides on a complex structure that reaches all the way to the core, 4,000 miles (6,436 kilometers) beneath our feet. The heat generated in the interior is enormous—in fact, part of our planet's core of iron exists in a molten state. There is too much heat generated for it to escape by the simple process of conduction (flowing out) through the rock. Instead, a layer of rock immediately underneath the earth's outer skin, the lithosphere—what scientists call the asthenosphere—actually melts and becomes liquid magma.

Even though the mantle is 2,000 miles (3,218 kilometers) thick and is made up almost entirely of rock, it responds to the heat much as a pot of water on a stove does when we turn on the heat. Hot columns of rock rise slowly to the top of the mantle, just underneath the outer crust, and give off their heat. Cooler columns of rock then descend into the interior to be heated and begin the cycle anew. The cycle is slow—it takes hundreds of millions of years to complete one loop. But it does succeed in carrying the earth's internal heat to the surface. On top of this hot interior, the earth's surface itself moves around, having no more influence on the forces that propel it than a leaf in a stream has on the currents that move it around.

One of the lighter of earth's solids is the granite (a light-colored rock that is formed when certain types of magma solidify underground) that makes up most of the continents. Slightly heavier is basaltic rock (darker rocks formed from magma that contains much iron and magnesium). The floor of the oceans is composed of basaltic rocks called gabbro and basalt. The continents "float" on heavier rock underneath the way pieces of wood float on water. Long ago, when our planet was newly formed, it was molten. Heavy materials, such as iron, sank to the center, while lighter materials floated to the top to form the early crust and lithosphere.

Below the crust, as we move toward the interior, the materials get progressively denser. The earth's crust is thicker under the continents, where it is about 25 miles (40 kilometers) thick. Beneath the crust is the mantle, extending down about 2,000 miles (3,218 kilometers). Beneath the mantle is the core, made almost entirely of iron and nickel. The outer layer of the core is molten, but the center, perhaps 790 miles (1,270 kilometers) in diameter, is solid metal.

All of these movements of the lithosphere and all of this heat contribute greatly to some violent phenomena on the surface of the earth, such as volcanic eruptions and earthquakes.

5

Our Shaking
Planet—Earthquakes

Every year, on the average, there are about 50,000 noticeable earthquakes all over the globe, and some estimates are that there are about a million small tremors every day. Most of these are minor and can be measured only with instruments. Still, the death toll from earthquakes is about 10,000 people annually. On the average, only one earthquake a year is classified as great. Eighteen are considered major and 120 are said to be strong. Great earthquakes measure 8 or more on the Richter scale; major quakes measure from 7 to 7.9; and strong tremors, 6 to 6.9.

The Richter scale is a measure of ground motion as recorded on seismographs, which are devices that operate with a heavy weight supported clear of the ground and freely suspended. When earthquake shock waves travel through the earth to the seismograph, they shake the supports on which the weight hangs. The weight, because of the inertia of its mass, tends to remain steady. A recording needle or pen that is attached to the weight traces a line on a revolving drum which is attached to the supports. The revolving drum shakes, and the pen records a zigzag line, showing the occurrence of an earthquake. The lines made by the pen make up what is called a seismogram.

The Richter scale is a measure of the energy given off from the point of origin of the quake, called the focus. The epicenter is the point on the earth's surface directly over the focus.

The Richter scale has no fixed maximum or minimum, and does not rate the size of a quake on a scale of ten. Each increase of one whole number means that the ground motion is ten times greater. And the energy released is about thirty-one times greater with each increasing value on the scale.

A reading of 3.5, for example, would probably mean slight, localized damage. A reading of 5 means a release of energy equivalent to an explosion of 1,000 tons (907,200 kilograms) of TNT. At 6, severe damage could result. One million tons (907,200,000 kilograms) of TNT would yield a reading of 7. Eight signifies a great quake that would cause tremendous damage. A reading of 2 is about the smallest that could be felt by a human being.

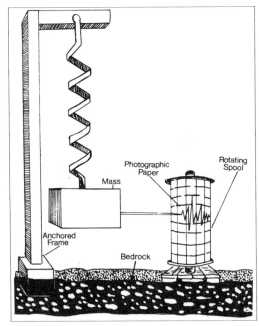

A diagram of the movement of a seismograph. The rotating spool vibrates during a quake. The light beam from a motionless pendulum makes a photo.

After the 1906 San Francisco earthquake. On foot and in carriages and wagons, San Franciscans crowd Market Street to view the still-smoldering ruins of the city's business district. In the distance, atop Nob Hill, is the Fairmont Hotel.

The Richter scale was devised by Charles Richter in 1935 and revised slightly in February 1977. The revision was made because over the years more sophisticated ways of measurement had been developed. The new scale didn't replace the old, but merely changed how quakes of the higher magnitude were recorded.

On October 1, 1987, a strong earthquake jolted the Los Angeles, California, area, killing at least six people, leaving twelve thousand homeless, and causing an estimated $150 million in damages. The epicenter was located on the north end of the Whittier fault, 7 miles southeast of Pasadena, and measured 6.1 on the Richter scale. The earthquake could be felt from San Luis Obispo, 160 miles (25.7 kilometers) northwest of Los Angeles, to the Mexican border, and as far east as Las Vegas, Nevada, 220 miles (322 kilometers) away.

Of our fifty states, Alaska and California appear to be the most vulnerable to severe quakes. One of the worst Alaskan earthquakes occurred in 1964 near Anchorage. It killed 131 people and was rated on the Richter Scale at 8.4. Indeed, it is predicted by scientists at Columbia University's Lamont-Doherty Geological Observatory that within twenty years a very large earthquake is likely to occur in a zone 125 to 150 miles (201 to 241 kilometers) long in the Shimagin Islands south of the Alaksan peninsula.

The area centers on a seismic gap, the Shimagin gap. A seismic gap is a portion of the subduction zone of known earthquakes that has not had a major quake in a long time; thus it is a region where a quake might be expected. The Shimagin gap is flanked on the east by a 150-mile (201-kilometer) zone that was ruptured in 1938 by an 8.2-magnitude earthquake. To the west is a shorter zone in which a 7.3-magnitude earthquake occurred in 1946. The Aleutian Islands and the Alaskan coast are subject to repeated earthquakes as the Pacific floor is subducted. When a quake has not occurred for many years in a portion of this seismic gap, it is assumed that tension has been building up and must be released by such an event.

As far as making the headlines in the United States, however, California is the champion. Here are the ten California earthquakes of the greatest magnitude in this century:

Site and Year	Magnitude
1. San Francisco, 1906	8.25
2. Kern County, 1952	7.8
3. Eureka, 1980	7.0
4. San Francisco, 1989	6.9
5. Coalinga, 1983	6.7
6. Imperial Valley, 1979	6.6
7. San Fernando Valley, 1971	6.4
8. Santa Barbara, 1925	6.3
9. Long Beach, 1933	6.3
10. Los Angeles, 1987	6.1

Most large earthquakes occur along what are known as faults. These are cracks or separations in rocks with vertical, horizontal, or both vertical and horizontal movements of the two sides relative to each other. In a fault, the usual pattern is that one side moves slowly in relationship to the other side. But sometimes there is not enough movement to relieve the forces building up under the ground. Then there is stress. The two sides readjust to each other, but there is so much stress that readjustment is rapid and violent. This is an earthquake.

Let us take a look at the lower 48 of the United States. A large part of the Pacific basin seems to be moving northwest in relationship to North America and Asia. It has stolen a slice of America, from Baja California (in Mexico) to San Francisco, and is dragging that slice with it. The edge of this slice is the San Andreas fault.

The San Andreas fault is some 995 miles (1,600 kilometers)

long, and it divides the Pacific and North American plates. The land on the east side of the fault is moving toward the south-southeast. On the western side, the land is going north-northwest. This causes stress to build up and the results may very well be an earthquake. And the San Andreas fault is not the only fault in California. There are about 2,000 miles (3,200 kilometers) of known faults which lace the state.

Almost everyone thinks of the lands east of the Rocky Mountains as gentle—at least as far as earthquakes are concerned. But each year about twenty quakes are felt in the eastern two-thirds of the country, where almost 85 percent of the U.S. population lives. Earthquakes in the eastern United States differ from those of the same magnitude in the western part of the country. Those in the East

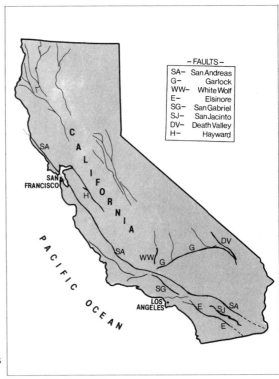

Coastal California is a mass of faults.

36

cause more damage, occur less frequently, and are felt over a much wider geographical area.

Indeed, the second and third worst earthquakes in the history of the United States occurred in the middle of the country. They happened in the New Madrid area in the southeastern part of Missouri in 1811 and 1812. They caused damage in Missouri, Kentucky, Tennessee, Ohio, Georgia, and South Carolina. Shocks were felt as far away as Boston, Massachusetts. Here are the ten earthquakes of the greatest magnitude in the lower 48 states:

Site and Date	Magnitude
1. San Francisco, Calif., April 18, 1906	8.25
2. New Madrid, Mo., February 7, 1812	8.2
3. New Madrid, Mo., December 16, 1811 (A.M.)	8.0
4. Fort Tejon, Calif., September 9, 1857	7.9
5. New Madrid, Mo., January 23, 1812	7.8
6. Owens Valley, Calif., March 26, 1872	7.8
7. Pleasant Valley, Nev., October 3, 1915	7.8
8. Kern County, Calif., July 21, 1952	7.8
9. Charleston, S. C., August 31, 1886	7.7
10. New Madrid, Mo., December 16, 1811 (P.M.)	7.6

There is an earthquake zone along the St. Lawrence River and the northwest border of New York State, to Lake Erie. Another zone follows the Mississippi Valley. New Englanders cannot be smug about quakes, either. There are at least three visible faults in Maine, three in New Hampshire, and one in Massachusetts. Fortunately, these are not in very heavily populated areas.

Earthquakes are common in many other countries, too. They seem to strike almost everywhere. On February 4, 1976, a quake shook Guatemala, killing 23,000 people and injuring 74,000. Almost a million were left homeless. This devastating quake was directly connected with plate activity in the region of the

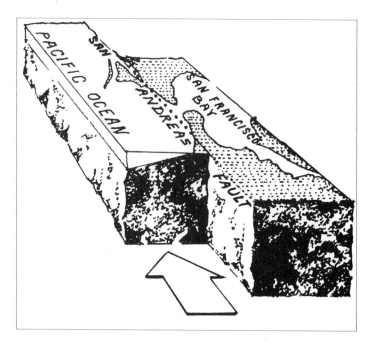

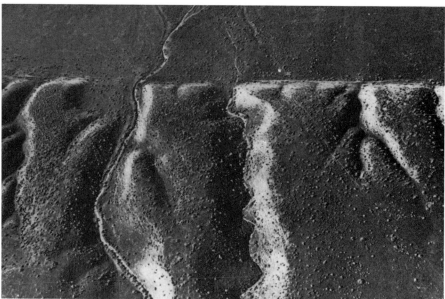

The diagram above shows the movement of the San Andreas Fault in the San Francisco Bay area. The photograph shows how displacement along the fault has caused visible changes in the directions of the two large watercourses.

Caribbean Sea and Central America. Central America, in fact, is located near the junction of three giant plates.

The western corner of the Caribbean plate, which carries most of the countries of Central America, appears to be caught in a wedge between the North American plate moving south-southeast and the Cocos plate moving northwest. The Caribbean plate, which is moving east, is gradually being torn apart. According to George Parker of the United States Geological Survey in Menlo Park, California, the action could result in the formation of an inland sea. This sea could stretch along the chain of volcanoes on the western side of Central America.

The Guatemalan earthquake in 1976 occurred on the Motagua fault, where the Caribbean and North American plates grind past each other. After sixty years of accumulating strain, the fault slipped and caused destruction and death.

Whatever else might happen, the countries of Guatemala, El Salvador, Honduras, and Nicaragua will probably be subject to earthquakes in the future. Movements along the fault system between the Caribbean and North American plates, movements of faults within the Caribbean plate, movement of the Cocos plate beneath the Caribbean plate, all cause earthquakes ranging from small to great.

On August 17, 1976, an earthquake struck the southeastern Philippine island of Mindanao, leaving 5,000 people dead and over 3,000 missing. About 150,000 people were without homes. The quake measured 7.8 on the Richter scale and was centered in the Celebes Sea, 500 miles (804 kilometers) south of the capital city of Manila and 100 miles (161 kilometers) east of Zamboanga City.

This particular quake was caused by movements between two great sections of the earth's lithosphere—the Indo-Australian and the Pacific plates. About 250 miles (402 kilometers) east of the quake's center lies the Philippine trench. Geologists believe that the trench is the place where the floor of the Pacific Ocean moves in a westward direction, subducting under the Philippine plate. The

Indo-Australian plate is pushing against the Himalaya Mountains from the south. Indeed, those very mountains were formed by plate movements. From the east, the Pacific plate is slipping under Japan at a rate of about 4 inches (10 centimeters) a year.

On July 28, 1976, there was an earthquake in Tangshan, China, that, it was thought, measured 8.2 on the Richter scale, although Chinese scientists did not release the statistics. The next day another occurred 70 miles (112.6 kilometers) north, near Beijing, that was reported at 7.9. An unofficial Chinese report was that the death toll in these two earthquakes was 665,000 and that 779,000 more had been injured.

The area of quakes in China was at a place where the earth's crust seems to be giving way to the pressures from the Indo-Australian

The results of an earthquake in Concepción, Chile.

plate. It was in that very area that the worst earthquake in history occurred, in 1556. That one killed more than 800,000 people.

After the Tangshan quake, Dr. Marcus Baath, the head of the Uppsala (Sweden) Seismological Institute, said that "between May and July, 1976, both the African and Indian landmasses have moved perceptively northward, pressing against Europe and the Himalayas respectively and causing a series of quakes."

Throughout history, China and Mongolia have been subjected to numerous earthquakes unlike those in many other parts of the world. Instead of following a definite fault line like the San Andreas fault in California, these Asian earthquakes are widely distributed.

By studying Asian tectonic plate movements and by examining satellite photographs of central Asia, two geologists, Peter Molnar and Paul Tapponnier of the Massachusetts Institute of Technology, developed a theory to explain the phenomenon, one that also suggests an eastern migration of China.

Some 120 million years ago, India began moving 4 to 7 inches (10.5 to 18 centimeters) northward each year from a position far to the south of its present one. The Himalayas were formed when the Indian landmass thrust itself into and under the Asian mass. But the collision did not stop India. This subcontinent, as a part of the Indo-Australian Plate, is still moving north about 2 inches (5.5 centimeters) each year.

The pressure of these two colliding plates has created a series of northwest-southeast oriented faults throughout Mongolia and China. Quakes result when India's movement forces parts of the Eurasian landmass to grind past each other at an angle. Because the enormous landmass to the west of China creates resistance, China and Mongolia have been pushed at least 310 miles (500 kilometers) to the east since the faulting began.

Of course, the United States, Central America, the Philippines, and China are not the only places where earthquakes occur. In that fateful year of 1976 there were three times more quakes measuring

8 or more on the Richter scale than during a normal year. In addition to the earthquakes in Guatemala, China, and the Philippines, many other places were hit.

On April 8, an earthquake measuring 7 on the Richter scale hit Uzbekistan in the Soviet Union. On May 6, the city of Udine, Italy, suffered a quake that measured 6.5, killed almost 1,000 people, injured more than 2,500 others, and left more than 100,000 homeless. On May 17, Uzbekistan was hit again by a quake that measured 7.2. And there were two quakes on May 29 at the Burma-China border, measuring 6.9 and 6.8.

On June 28, West New Guinea suffered a horrible earthquake measuring 7.2, which killed 7,000 people. On July 14, a quake on the island of Bali measured 5.6, killed 440 people, and injured 3,000. On August 18, a moderate earthquake jolted the central part of Honshu, Japan's main island. Another hit the southwestern part of Turkey on August 19. In November, earthquakes shook Iran, the Philippines again, Greece, and Japan again—all on the first weekend of the month. And many of these occurred in areas that also contain volcanoes.

6

The Earth in Uproar—
Volcanoes and Hotspots

When two lithosperic plates are pushed together, one may slide under the other. This process, called subduction, creates both earthquakes and volcanoes. As the plate taking the nosedive goes deeper and deeper, it starts to melt. The molten rock, less dense than the solid rock surrounding it, pushes up and melts through cracks, and may spew out as a volcano. Mount St. Helens and Mount Shasta on the west coast of the United States, as well as the volcanoes of Japan, are examples of such volcanoes.

Subduction causes earthquakes because the plates don't slide smoothly past each other. They may stick for many years at a time, then jolt forward all at once. Some earthquake faults, like the San Andreas, are not associated with volcanoes because the two plates are simply moving past each other in a sidewise motion. Neither of the plates is sliding deep into the earth and melting.

Throughout the entire world, there are about 760 known active volcanoes. Of these, 95 in recorded history have been known to cause casualties. In that fateful year of 1976, 10 of them were active, but that number rose to 35 in 1977, when Japan had 14 disastrous eruptions, Java in Indonesia had 12, and the Philippines and Central America had 6 each.

What causes them? As the plates move, drifting apart and colliding with each other, faults are created, and this is where trouble can occur. As the plates separate, magma, the molten material, rises to fill the rift in a midocean ridge. Where the plates collide or ride up on each other, volcanoes can occur on the overriding plate.

For example, as the Pacific seafloor squeezes under the continental rims at subduction zones, the molten magma can rise and break through the earth's crust. This has created volcanoes all around the Pacific Ocean, a circle of volcanoes called the Ring of Fire. It runs along the Aleutian Islands, down the coast of Japan, through the Philippines, Indonesia, New Caledonia, and northern New Zealand to the west coast of South America, and up Central America and Mexico to the Cascade Range in Oregon, Washington, and northern California.

The crater of a volcano in Costa Rica.

Mediterranean volcanoes, such as Vesuvius, Etna, and Stromboli, are caused in somewhat the same way. There are many colliding plates with their embedded continents surrounding the Mediterranean. As the African plate met the Eurasian plate, it jammed Italy into Europe, creating the Alps. Spain pivoted southward, pinching up the Pyrenees Mountains as it tore away from the Atlantic coast of France. Turkey, pushed westward by the Arabian plate, invaded the Aegean Sea.

Because of their nature and the way they erupt, some volcanoes are more dangerous than others. The most terrible of all volcanic eruptions is the glowing avalanche, or *nuée ardente*. This is a volcanic eruption in which extremely hot liquids, solids, and gases flow rapidly down the sides of a volcanic mountain. It occurs with the speed of an explosion and is hot enough to kill instantly. The heat is so great that any living thing in its path is burned to a crisp.

Lava flows occur when volumes of fluid lava (molten rock above ground) pour out of the fissures of the volcanic cone. Heavy flows, called flood eruptions, are very damaging. They can knock out communications and destroy property and farmland. Mudflows, caused by heavy rainstorms or a melting glacier during an eruption, can also be quite destructive. They can move down the slopes of a volcano at speeds high enough to carry large boulders and they can crush anything in their paths.

Oddly enough, there are volcanoes that seem to have nothing to do with the edges of the plates. A good example of this is the line of volcanoes that compose the Hawaiian Islands. The entire Hawaiian Island chain, from end to end, contains more than 50 volcanoes both above and below the surface of the Pacific Ocean. Where they came from puzzled early plate technologists.

First of all, the ocean floor on which the mountain chain is located is a lot older than the island chain itself—80 million years older near the Big Island of Hawaii and 95 million years older past the Midway Islands. Second, these volcanoes do not stand where the theory of plate tectonics predicted they would be. They are not at the edges of plates—either where the plates are spreading, as along the midocean ridge, or where they are colliding, as in Japan. Instead, they are located squarely in the middle of the Pacific plate.

In the 1960s, J. Tuzo Wilson, the Canadian scientist who was one of the founders of the theory of plate tectonics, thought that convection in the mantle produced what other scientists later called a hotspot, or plume. The Hawaiian Islands had arisen from magma poking through the seafloor as it moved over the hotspot. So the seafloor had formed millions of years earlier and a long distance farther east.

Later, W. Jason Morgan of Princeton University came up with the idea of a sort of "thunderhead" of concentrated energy beneath the Big Island of Hawaii, welling up from deep within

Even a small volcano can produce a great deal of lava.

the earth. It was likened to a huge blowtorch that built up one volcano after another as the plate moved over the plume. Meantime, the volcanic mountains were taken away like newly baked cupcakes on a conveyor belt. He also believed that a hotspot is almost stationary.

Nowhere on earth does the hotspot theory seem quite so well documented as in the Hawaiian Island chain. Indeed, it is on the Big Island of Hawaii where one of the most extensive volcano forecasting installations can be found. The observatory is on the rim of the volcano Kilauea, the world's most active volcano, and near Mauna Loa, a volcano that may erupt at any time. Mauna Loa, Hawaiian for Long Mountain, is the largest (by volume) mountain on earth. It rises 13,680 feet (4,300 meters) above sea level, and its dome measures 75 miles by 64 miles (121 by 103 kilometers).

A solidified lava field in Hawaii.

But Hawaii is not the only place where hotspots can be found. The earth seems to be peppered with them. Wilson, using the most basic definition of a hotspot—volcanism far from plate edges— listed just a few, all in the oceans. Morgan upped the list to about 20. Most scientists now think that there are more than 120 hotspots. Their lists include some likely hotspots under Africa and Europe, in the United States under Yellowstone National Park and, in the oceans, under the Azores Islands west of Spain and Portugal, the Society Islands (Tahiti is the main island), and the Galápagos Islands off the western coast of South America.

These hotspots might be a part of the engine that drives the moving plates. As magma from the lower mantle wells up toward the surface, much of it never gets there. Instead, according to Morgan, the magma fans out under the plate, buoying the plate up and helping to push it past the hotspot.

A rift on Kilauea.

7

The Earth in Motion—Slipping, Sliding, and Colliding

Scientists believe that our earth is unique in our solar system. This is because, unlike the other planets in the solar system, it is still in the process of being born. It is still forming itself. The main reason for this belief is that mountains are still forming on our planet. Other planets, such as Venus, Mars, and Mercury have mountains, but they are not believed to be growing because the planets cooled off long ago and their internal heat engines have stopped working. Our mountains, like everything else on earth, are born, live out their lives, and disappear, to be replaced by new mountains.

According to the theory of plate tectonics, each plate acts mostly as a rigid unit, usually changing only at its edges. The edges, or margins, between plates can diverge (separate), converge (come together), or slide past each other. But very little changes in the middle of the plate. In fact, some of the earth's most violent events, such as earthquakes and volcanic eruptions, define the boundaries of the main plates.

At midocean ridges, the plate edges diverge as magma, rising from the asthenosphere, adds new plate material. The ridges are mountains composed of chains of numerous volcanoes and lava flows. Along their length, shallow earthquakes, less than 30 miles (50 kilometers) below the surface, are common.

In zones where the plates move past each other, the boundaries are said to be sliding. Little plate material is added or destroyed at these faults, but they are associated with shallow earthquakes, sometimes very strong ones. The San Andreas fault of California is a classic example of sliding plate boundaries.

Where two plates converge, or collide, a deep trench forms and one plate is subducted downward into the asthenosphere, sliding deeply below the other, returning old plate material to the asthenosphere. At these boundaries, mountains form and chains of islands, called island arcs, appear. Earthquakes occur at a range of depths, down to 435 miles (700 kilometers), along the descend-

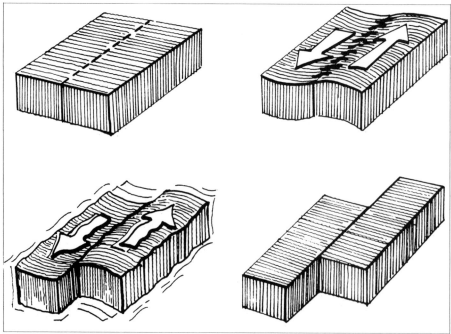

Slippage along a fault. Upper left: The blocks are at rest. Upper right: Stress forms deformation. Lower left: The blocks rupture. Lower right: The blocks rest again.

ing plate. Typical examples of the activity at converging plates are the Andes Mountains of western South America and the Aleutian Islands of Alaska.

Great mountain ranges are often the outcome of an ocean plate converging with a thick continental plate. The edge of the continent acts rather like the cutting edge of a carpenter's plane. It shaves great masses of material from the top of the ocean plate as it descends into the asthenosphere. Slowly, the shavings build up to form mountains. Much of the descending ocean plate is reabsorbed into the asthenosphere. Some of the lighter material, during melting, rises up and swells the growing mountains by creating a "root" beneath them. If this magma forces its way to the surface, the result is a range of volcanoes like the Cascade Range in the western United States.

Finally, two plates with continents at their edges may collide. The rocks on the continents are of relatively low density and too buoyant to descend into the asthenosphere. The result is a huge zone of crushing, where rocks and other materials are folded, overthrust, and welded together. This is how massive mountain chains such as the Himalayas emerged.

Collisions were the cause of the formation of much of what was to become North America. More than 300 million years ago, Europe and Africa began to collide with North America. This was at the time that the supercontinent Pangea was forming. As these collisions occurred, a block of crust was working its way up the eastern shore of North America in the same way as another block of crust would later do on the western coast. The Appalachian Mountain chain had begun to form.

By Permian times, about 290 million years ago, these mountains were high and mighty, probably as imposing as the Himalayas are today. The collisions formed an overthrust belt (a location where rocks have slid over other rocks at a low angle during mountain building) that runs for 1,100 miles (1,800

The subcontinent of India, originally attached to what is now Antarctica, made the longest migration of all the drifting landmasses—about 5,600 miles (9,000 kilometers) in 200 million years.

kilometers) along eastern North America, much of it stretching from Pennsylvania to Alabama.

Europe also exhibits the effect of continental collision. The Alps, the Apennines, and the Carpathian mountain ranges were caused by collisions that folded and twisted the hard "solid" stone. The layers of stone in the Alps, for example, were originally formed under the sea and later bent to form the mountains. The rock has never melted, yet one can see it folded into loops on the cliff faces of peak after peak. Rock is plastic and will bend under some combination of heat, pressure, and time. All three are at work deep inside a mountain range.

In the Mediterranean basin, several small plates located between the African and Eurasian plates have been, and are now, crashing, separating, rotating, subducting, and grinding into one another. Their continuing collision and subduction have caused earthquakes and volcanism for centuries. They have buried Pompeii and blown up the Greek island of Santorini, and earthquakes and volcanoes continue to occur in Greece, Algeria, Italy, Romania, Yugoslavia, and Morocco.

8

A Word of Caution

Nearly all earth scientists now believe in the theory of continental drift and plate tectonics. But in all fairness, it should be pointed out that there are still those who are disbelievers. Many of them are brilliant, educated scientists, and we should pay attention to what they have to say. One of the most distinguished of the doubters is Paul D. Lowman, Jr. A veteran geologist in the geophysics branch of NASA's Goddard Space Flight Center, whose chief area of research is crustal evolution, he also planned NASA's Crustal Dynamics Program.

Lowman pointed out that continental drift has not really been measured, simply because until recently scientists have not had the tools. We can now do this, using radio telescopes and laser-tracking satellites, but it will be some years before we have enough data to prove whether or not the continents actually do move.

He agreed that the continental boundaries do match, but he pointed out that when the jigsaw puzzle is fitted together, there are holes and extra pieces left behind. For example, in the Mid-Atlantic Ridge, which extends into the Arctic Ocean, there is seismic activity that shows clearly that the seafloor is spreading.

So landmasses on either side of the Arctic Ocean, such as Canada and the Soviet Union, should have been pushed apart, leaving similar margins. Depth maps of the Arctic Ocean, however, do not show parallel edges, much less a precise fit.

Lowman also found some leftover land. Supposedly the Atlantic Ocean was closed hundreds of millions of years ago by the nestling of the east coast of North America against the west coast of Europe. But if this were so, there would be no room for a large part of southern Mexico. This piece, he said, could not have formed since the opening of the Atlantic because much of southern Mexico is very much older crust.

He questioned the fit of the puzzle itself. He agreed that the continents fit together quite well, but argued that a case could also be made for a good fit between western South America and Australia. This, he said, indicates that the Pacific might be widening instead of shrinking—and, if both the Atlantic and Pacific oceans are widening, then the earth itself must be expanding. This would mean that as the earth expanded, its rotation should slow down because of its increased volume. Yet geologists have evidence that the earth's day has increased by only two hours over the last 370 million years. "In short," he wrote, "the expanding Earth theory is stimulating, but quite unlikely."

Then there were the discoveries of plants and animals and their fossils on widely separated continents. Lowman offered expert testimony that some of the animals may have been better swimmers than was thought and that some of the plants had winglike spores that could easily be spread by the wind over hundreds of miles. He also felt that there should be many more similar fossils on separate continents than have been found up to now.

Lowman also cited some other evidence from geophysicists. They said that there is no asthenosphere under most continents, or at best a poorly developed, very deep one—250 miles (400 kilometers) or more deep. Without an effective plastic asthenosphere, he wondered, how can continents move?

As to hotspots, he said that they should be found on continents as well as in the oceans. He pointed out that some scientists have indicated that their study of the distribution of volcanoes in North Africa, they found no hotspot trails. That made them conclude that the African continent had stayed in the same place for some 25 million years.

Lowman concluded with a reasoned statement:

> I propose plate tectonics with fixed continents instead of plate tectonics and continental drift. . . . Very few geologists today can deny the essential processes of plate tectonics—seafloor spreading, subduction, and transform faulting. They have all, geophysically speaking, been observed. Continental drift, in contrast, depends heavily on incomplete or conflicting evidence. Only a widening gap between continents would serve as direct evidence for drift. If no one finds the Atlantic broadening soon, perhaps plate tectonic theory will no longer carry continental drift as a necessary passenger. Still, the quest for more information about plate tectonics goes on. Geologists are hunting the world for rifts, faults, spreading zones, and possible new volcanoes—getting from the rocks the story of where they have been and where they are going.

There are many mysteries to solve. We still don't know exactly what drives the plates. Most experts think it is convection in the mantle, but some believe gravity is the major cause of plate movement as denser plates sink and pull the rest of the plate with them. We still don't know what hotspots really are, and what their true role is in the geological pattern of change. We still don't know if we can use our knowledge of plate tectonics to solve our energy and environmental problems or to predict earthquakes and volcanic eruptions. Will we ever learn the secrets of our earth's beginnings?

But as the renowned marine geologist and geophysicist, Robert D. Ballard, once wrote:

> Whatever it is that moves the plates, we should hope that it continues. For when it stops—when mountains no longer wring out the clouds nor volcanoes rejuvenate the soil—then the mountains will wash into the sea, never to return, and the face of our world will again be "without form, and void." And so we have the central paradox of our living planet—that its most violent and destructive forces make life possible on its face.

Glossary

asthenosphere—The semisolid layer of earth below the lithosphere, part of the upper mantle.

basalt—Dark rock formed by the cooling of molten lava and composed of large amounts of dense iron and magnesium.

continental drift—An early theory that the continents somehow moved across the surface of the earth—replaced by the theory of plate tectonics after the discovery of seafloor spreading.

convection current—A circular current caused by the movement of heated material through a fluid. Colder, denser materials sink, causing warmer, less dense materials to rise.

core—The iron and nickel center of the earth. A liquid outer core surrounds the solid inner core.

convergence—The collision of two lithospheric plates.

crust—The outermost shell or layer of the earth, the upper part of the lithosphere.

divergence—The separating or spreading of two lithospheric plates.

epicenter—The point on the earth's surface directly above the focus of an earthquake.

fault—A crack in crustal rocks, the sides of which move against each other.

focus—The place in the earth where an earthquake begins.

geologist—A scientist who studies the earth—its composition, origin, history, and the processes that alter it, such as streams and glaciers.

geyser—A spring that occasionally erupts hot water and steam.

granite—Light-colored rock, composed mainly of visible pieces of quartz and feldspar, that forms when certain types of magma solidify underground.

guyot—A flat-topped seamount.

hotspot—A semipermanent heat source of rising magma in the mantle that causes volcanism; also called a plume.

lava—Molten rock above ground or molten rock above ground after it solidifies.

lithosphere—The solid, outermost shell of the earth. It includes the crust and the uppermost part of the mantle.

magma—Liquid rock materials and dissolved gases beneath the surface of the earth.

mantle—The thick layer of earth between the crust and the outer core.

mesosphere—The section of the earth between the asthenosphere and the core—part of the mantle.

midocean ridge—A chain of volcanic islands and lava flows, largely under water and found in the ocean basins at plate-spreading zones.

nuée ardente—An extremely hot type of volcanic eruption that looks like a glowing avalanche.

Pangaea—The supercontinent that existed about 200,000,000 to 300,000,000 years ago, when all land areas were connected. The present continents were formed by separating from Pangaea.

plate—One of the segments that makes up the earth's lithosphere.

plate tectonics—The theory that the earth's lithosphere is made up of separate pieces, or plates, which migrate over the plastic mantle layer (the asthenosphere).

pumice—A volcanic glassy rock containing many small bubbles.

Richter scale—A measure of the ground motion of earthquakes that indicates the amount of energy released by an earthquake.

rift—A gap in the surface of the earth formed when two blocks of crust move apart.

seamount—An undersea volcanic mountain taller than 3,300 feet (1,000 meters) that is common at midocean ridges.

seismograph—A device used to measure and record the ground motion of an earthquake.

subduction—The descent of one plate beneath another.

transform fault—A type of fault, usually crossing the midocean ridge at a right angle and separating one segment of the ridge from the next.

underthrusting—Any process by which a lower block of rock moves under an upper block of rock.

Further Reading

Anderson, Alan H. *The Drifting Continents*. New York: Putnam, 1971.

Asimov, Isaac. *How Did We Find Out About Volcanoes?* New York: Avon Books, 1987.

Aylesworth, Thomas G. *Geological Disasters*. New York: Franklin Watts, 1979.

Aylesworth, Thomas G., and Stanley Klein. *Science Update '77*. Syracuse, N.Y.: Gaylord Professional Publications, 1977.

————. *Science Update '78*. Syracuse, N.Y.: Gaylord Professional Publications, 1978.

Ballard, Robert D. *Exploring Our Living Planet*. Washington, D.C.: National Geographic Society, 1983.

Curran, Eileen. *Mountains and Volcanoes*. Mahwah, N.J.: Troll, 1985.

Geological Museum (London). *Earthquakes*. New York: Cambridge University Press, 1986.

Glen, William. *Continental Drift and Plate Tectonics*. Columbus, Ohio: Merrill, 1975.

Golden, Frederic. *The Trembling Earth*. New York: Charles Scribner, 1987.

Hallam, A. *A Revolution in the Earth Sciences: From Continental Drift to Plate Tectonics*. London: Oxford University Press, 1973.

Harrington, John W. *The Dance of the Continents*. Los Angeles: J.P. Tarcher, 1983.

Hiscock, Bruce. *The Big Rock*. New York: Atheneum, 1988.

Holden, John C. *Earth in Motion*. New York: Morrow, 1978.

Kiefer, Irene. *Global Jigsaw Puzzle*. New York: Atheneum, 1978.

Marvin, Ursula B. *Continental Drift: The Evolution of a Concept.* Washington, D.C.: Smithsonian Institution Press, 1972.

McConnell, Anita. *The World Beneath Us*. New York: Facts on File, 1986.

Miller, Russell. *Continents in Collision*. Arlington, Va.: Time-Life Books, 1983.

Raymo, Chet. *The Crust of Our Earth*. Englewood Cliffs, N.J.: Prentice-Hall, 1983.

Simon, Seymour. *Volcanoes*. New York: Morrow, 1988.

Sullivan, Walter. *Continents in Motion*. New York: McGraw-Hill Book Co., 1974.

Tarling, Don and Maureen. *Continental Drift*. Garden City, N.Y.: Anchor Books, 1975.

Thackray, John. *Age of the Earth*. New York: Cambridge University Press, 1986.

van Rose, Susanna, and Ian Mercer. *Volcanoes*. New York: Cambridge University Press, 1986.

Weiss, Malcolm E. *Lands Adrift*. New York: Parents Magazine Press, 1975.

Index